PREVENTING PUPP

Live in peace with

Dee Woodcock

CONTENTS

PART ONE: LIVE IN PEACE WITH YOUR PUPPY

Making your choice	page 1
Those early days	page 3
Crate training	page 3
House training	page 5
Feeding the puppy	page 7
Socialisation	page 8
Coping with a fear response	page 12
Using rewards	page 12
House rules - setting the boundaries	page 13
Think about everyday situations	page 16
Teaching your puppy those basic cues - using lure/reward or clicker training	page 20
Canine communication	page 26
More than just a game	page 29

PART TWO: COPING WITH COMMON PROBLEMS

Pulling on lead	page 31
Jumping up	page 32
Play biting	page 33
Food bowl training	page 34
Begging at table	page 36
Home alone	page 37
Barking	page 37
Barking in the car	page 38
Don't snatch!	page 38
Stealing food	page 39
Stealing socks...and other things	page 40
Grooming	page 40
Fear of other dogs	page 41
Fear of visitors	page 42
Safety with children	page 43
Introducing other pets	page 44
Digging	page 46
Car sickness	page 46
Chewing	page 47
Taking possession of the sofa	page 48
Recall problems	page 48

PREVENTING PUPPY PROBLEMS

PART ONE: LIVE IN PEACE WITH YOUR PUPPY

MAKING YOUR CHOICE

Puppies! Delightful, enchanting, cuddly, exhilarating, charming, exhausting, maddening, and an absolute joy. Puppies are all of those things, and more. Puppies are designed by nature to delight from the second you set eyes on them. What prettier sight is there than a litter of four or five week old puppies bumbling happily about, tripping over each other, chewing each other, running, playing, and falling into deep sudden sleep?

And here comes your first big decision. Which is the right puppy for you? Perhaps you already have a favourite breed, or one or two that appeal. Talk to owners; most will be more than willing to extol the virtues of their breed. Visit some shows if possible, and see examples of the breed from puppy through to adult. Find a reputable breeder through the Kennel Club, or through personal recommendation.

You may be seeking a litter bred and reared at home, or you may choose to go to kennels which have specialised in your chosen breed for some years. Often you will read advice which suggests you only buy a home bred puppy. The fact is that there are not hundreds and hundreds of puppies being born and raised in households, and though this might well be the ideal start, there is no problem with a kennel bred puppy providing some regular gentle handling and good socialisation have begun.

Kennel bred puppies will - in the main - be the product of knowledgeable breeding over some generations. Home bred puppies are often carefully bred, but sometimes the puppies are the result of two dogs mated about which the owners actually know very little. Whichever you choose, ask a lot of questions and be prepared to be asked just as many. A caring breeder will be seeking good, permanent loving homes for her carefully bred and reared litter. Visit the litter twice if possible, first at about five weeks old, and again ten to fourteen days later so that you can see how they are developing.

Meet the puppies' mother, and ensure she has a calm and pleasant temperament. Keep in mind that she will be concerned for the safety of her puppies, so a little natural caution as you approach is normal. But be aware too that if she is snappy, irritable, or aggressive, her puppies may well have inherited or learned the same kind of responses. She may look a little untidy as bitches tend to drop their coat after raising their litter, and she may also look a little thin. But she should be friendly, willing to come to you, and look healthy and well cared for, even if her coat is a little raggy and she has lost some condition through feeding and caring well for her puppies.

Look for warm, cosy living conditions, with space in which the puppies are able to play, and check that there are toys and play things available for them. It's important that they have had things to stimulate them mentally, as well as space to run about and play together. The run should be reasonably clean, but keep in mind that puppies do urinate and defecate frequently. Ask if they have been handled regularly, and if they have met other people, and children. Are there other animals, cats perhaps, resident in the house or at the kennels? Have they been introduced to household sounds? This too is important - a washing machine suddenly starting up or a hoover rushing over the carpet towards a small puppy can be a frightening first time experience.

Ask to see the pedigree certificates of both the dam and the sire, and check that they are Kennel Club registered. If they are not, then your puppy cannot be registered either. That may be no problem to you, but if you plan to breed or show the puppy then it is essential that he can be registered. Keep in mind too that an unregistered puppy has less value and this fact should be reflected in the purchase price. Ask also to see copies of any test certificates for both parents, relating to hereditary defects, if relevant to your breed.

Physically your puppy should be plump without being fat. Avoid puppies with a "pot-bellied" appearance as this might indicate a heavy burden of worms. He should be bright-eyed, his nose free of any discharge, his skin should be clean, his coat free of parasites, and he should be willing to approach you to be stroked.

Time spent now in checking all these seemingly dry-as-dust details is the first step on the road to preventing puppy problems.

A carefully bred puppy, reared in good conditions, handled regularly and given mental and physical stimulation will cope much better with the transition to his new home. An additional bonus is that he will also be able to cope much better with all those little surprises life has in store for him in the human world.

And so you fall in love, choose the one for you and bring him home at eight weeks. At this stage he is still a cuddly bundle, with knobbly knees and feet too large for the rest of him. But it's an indisputable fact that puppies GROW. And they grow very quickly indeed. One day you have an enthusiastic puppy who comes hot foot to find you, or who indulges in some energetic puppy play with you, and then keels over into deep peaceful sleep. In a very short time you have a much larger and even more energetic puppy and he is into mischief with a vengeance.

THOSE EARLY DAYS

Now the most familiar cry will be "Where's the puppy?" and the answer will probably be in just about the last place you want him to be! Now is the time when eyes in the back of your head would be a real advantage, but failing that, the sensible approach is to make sure that you have considerable time to spend with the puppy - he really needs time and attention in those first few vital weeks. You and he have to get to know one another, you begin to build the bond between you, house training will be in progress, you will be beginning to teach him to respond to you, and of course you and he need time to play together. These are busy and pleasurable weeks.

In the times when you cannot be available to keep an eye on him, be prepared to confine him in a smaller space or use a crate so that you are certain he is not up to mischief. Even more important, you can be certain he is not chewing something which may injure him. Introduction to the crate is a key issue, and it is described in detail in the following section.

CRATE TRAINING

The initial response of many people when using a crate is mentioned is to shudder and say "how cruel". Yes, a crate can be used abusively, but it can also be a safe haven and a great place for a puppy to be. Keep in mind that dogs are den animals, and most are very comfortable in a confined area. The key to the puppy resting peacefully in his crate lies in getting one of the right size, and most of all, in the way it is introduced to him.

The crate should be big enough to allow him to lay full length and to stand comfortably, keeping in mind that puppies grow very quickly indeed. What may look ridiculously large when he is eight weeks old tends to shrink by the time he is five or six months old! So think big rather than small.

Put bedding inside the crate, plus some toys and a few small food treats. Encourage the puppy to go inside by tossing in some treats or tossing in a toy, and LEAVE THE DOOR OPEN. If you shut the door too soon, you will have a puppy whining and distressed. Once the puppy goes in and out of his own accord, then close the door for just a few minutes. Build on the time it is used, but be careful not to release the puppy if he is whining or barking, or he will quickly learn that barking brings you running to release him.

The crate can be used in the house for short periods while you are cooking, ironing, or dishing up meals - at any time really when the puppy could easily get underfoot and be injured. It can be used when you have to go out and leave him for short periods, and it can be used as a safe travelling area in the car.

It is also an aid in house training as puppies rarely soil their sleeping area, but keep in mind a very young puppy cannot be expected to hold on for long periods. Ensure he has an opportunity to empty bowel and bladder before putting him in the crate, and release him to go outside after he has had a sleep.

Extend the length of time for which the puppy is left in the crate starting with just a few minutes - unless he falls asleep of course, in which case leave him to rest. Keep in mind he should never be left in the crate for more than two hours, and then only when he is used to the crate and settles happily in it.

Never be tempted to put him in the crate when you are angry. If you use the crate as a place of punishment, the puppy will quickly cease to see it as a safe place to be.

HOUSE TRAINING

Probably more is written about house training than any other subject. Yet it is one of the easiest things to teach your puppy, and even an older dog who has never lived in a house can be trained in this way. House training begins as soon as the puppy arrives at his new home. If you are able to spend two or three days paying a great deal of attention to the puppy you will very soon realise that:

- he will usually urinate within minutes of waking
- he will usually urinate after being fed
- he will usually empty his bowel within 10-15 minutes of being fed

It is absolutely essential that if the puppy has an accident in the house, he is not punished or shouted at. This serves only to make him hide away, and you may find puddles behind chairs or sofas.

Take the puppy to the place in the garden you have decided he is to use, and stay with him until he obliges. He may simply wander about and sniff, but be patient. Staying with him is important. If you put the puppy outside, he may well do nothing, come back into the house and wet the carpet. The second he empties, he is just the world's best puppy (well of course he is anyway). Praise him to the skies and give him a small food reward. Never underestimate the value of food rewards when training. Food is essential to survival and even the tiniest puppy is programmed to strive for survival. It is a potent reward for most puppies, and for most dogs too.

It is very useful to have a word that you use when you want the puppy to empty. Remember to make it one you are willing to use in public! At first you say the chosen word when you see he is beginning to empty, and follow it with praise and a treat. Once learned, this is useful if you are dashing out in a hurry and want to be sure your puppy is comfortable in your absence.

Take the puppy outside every hour in the first few days. Puppies are naturally clean and most will not soil their own bed. If he has to be left for a while, then the use of a crate is sensible because almost certainly the puppy will not soil there. He should not of course be expected to hold on for three or four hours in the first few weeks. His bladder is very small at this stage.

You will need to give some thought to how you will cope at night. No puppy can be expected to be clean through the night until at least 12 weeks of age - some take longer, some will be a little quicker. An easy way to cope in those first few weeks, is to sleep the puppy in a large cardboard box near your bed, or in his crate if you are using one. When he wakes he will scrabble about and you can quickly take him outside (yes, I know, it's cold and dark but it will be worth it!). Praise and reward him when he obliges.

If the puppy has to be left for several hours, and you are not using a crate, then confine him to a reasonably small area in kitchen or utility room, and ensure that he has had the opportunity to eliminate before you leave. He should not need to empty again for two hours or so. It may seem tempting to lay newspaper for him to go on, but here you would be effectively teaching him that it is acceptable to eliminate indoors - the absolute opposite of what you want him to do. This gives conflicting messages, and usually delays the process of house training. If you feel he cannot hold on for the length of time you will be absent, then put a shallow box with a piece of turf inside it (if the puppy usually empties on grass) near his bedding, and you should find he will use this in your absence. Remember clean water should always be available. Reducing water intake will not prevent the puppy urinating - but lack of water can make him seriously ill quite quickly.

If your puppy is not reasonably reliable by about sixteen weeks, then look again at the training methods you are using. Is somebody punishing him for accidents? Is he given enough opportunities to go outside? Is the praise and reward generous? Remember that puppies leave their sleeping place to eliminate as early as three weeks old - all we do is teach them the appropriate place to go.

Using these methods usually results in a puppy that is house trained very quickly. Three or four days of this can result in a puppy that asks to go outside in the day time but every puppy is different, so be patient and don't expect too much too soon. You may be lucky and have a puppy that is reliable very quickly, but then find he still has the occasional accident. Ignore any accidents that occur, clean up when the puppy is elsewhere, and promise yourself you will take him outside more frequently.

It is important to clean soiled areas thoroughly as soon as possible after the accident happens. An ammonia based cleaner should not be used - urine smells of ammonia, and the puppy will be attracted back to the same spot time and time again. A solution of hot water and a biological washing powder works well, or your veterinary surgeon can supply a purpose-made cleaner.

FEEDING THE PUPPY

Following on concerns about house training, feeding probably takes next priority in what can cause you, as a new owner, to worry. It is not unusual for a puppy who was eating well among his litter mates to go off his food for two or three days after joining his new family. Everything is strange, and of course there are no litter mates to provide competition for the food.

This is the point when it is easy to rush out and buy five different sorts of food, or even cut up your Sunday roast, in the hope of tempting that capricious appetite. But resist the temptation. No puppy will ever starve himself if there is food available. If you have a cat in the house, you may well find he will try to share the cat's food, but that is designed for cats, so persuade him gently back to his own bowl and move the cat's to a higher level.

If you do not like the food the breeder has raised the puppies on, then by all means change to another puppy food. Take at least five days and preferably more to change gradually from one to the other. Otherwise you may find your puppy has a very upset stomach.

There is a wide choice of puppy foods available now, ranging from canned food, which is mixed with puppy grade biscuit meal, through to complete foods which provide all the puppy needs, and to which you need add nothing. The ingredients vary widely, and so do the prices. Like most things, you get what you pay for. A food offering good quality meat or poultry protein is more easily digested than one providing cereal as its main ingredient. It may look more expensive, but if you do the calculations, you will find that you feed less of a good quality protein food and thus it costs little or no more.

An alternative is to provide a home prepared diet, either of raw meat with vegetables and rice, or cooked meat with vegetables and rice. This has become increasingly popular in recent years, but it does need some careful calculation and if this is your choice, it would be wise to obtain one of the very good books published solely on the topic of the Natural Diet.

An eight week old puppy is fed four times daily, around 7 am, midday, 5 pm, and 9 pm, but times can be chosen to suit yourself. Puppies grow very rapidly, so quantities need to be increased steadily. At twelve weeks of age, meals are reduced to three daily again with increased quantity, and this pattern remains until the puppy is six months old. At that stage meals can be reduced to two larger ones daily.

Meal times do not need to be set in stone, but keep in mind that if the puppy is fed at regular intervals, he will also eliminate at regular intervals, so it does aid house training to keep to a fairly regular schedule.

SOCIALISATION

Now we come to the magic word which entered into dog owning language back in the 1990's. Socialisation! What does it actually mean?

Socialisation simply means introducing the puppy as young as possible to as many experiences as possible, taking care that each experience is pleasant and rewarding. Puppies begin to learn as early as five weeks of age, so when he joins his new family at eight weeks old, he is already half way into his peak learning period. This takes place between four weeks and twelve weeks of age.

This very rapid learning period begins to diminish at around sixteen weeks, and by eighteen weeks the puppy may refuse to cooperate in actions that he has previously carried out willingly. This is the age at which many owners become very despondent about the progress of their puppy. This is also the period in which the puppy develops a fear/flight response, during which he will take longer to accept new experiences. The time taken to learn increases as he gets older, but of course he learns throughout life. (Yes, you can teach an old dog new tricks - it just takes longer!).

Socialisation should start immediately the puppy joins his family, and hopefully the breeder will already have done some work on this before then. He needs to be introduced to as many people as possible, including children and babies even if there are none in the family at that time. You need to think about introducing him to all different kinds of people, different kinds of clothing, hats, umbrellas, shopping bags, walking sticks, wheelchairs, baby buggies, people in crash helmets, cycles, skateboards, traffic noises, travelling in the car, the shopping centre, station, grooming parlour if the puppy is a breed than needs professional grooming, the veterinary surgery and the pub if your local is one that allows dogs. Take him on a bus, on a train, in a lift, sit in the station letting a few trains go by. He needs to meet other dogs, cats, and other animals. The more situations the puppy meets in his early months the better balanced he will be and better able to cope with what life throws at him.

Make sure that the puppy is accustomed to walking along busy roads where he takes in the sight, smell and noise of traffic. Never mind that you never intend to take him along a busy road - a house move at a later date might involve living on or close to a road which is heavily used by traffic. Start off with quiet side roads and build up to busier ones. Bicycles can be terrifying to a puppy. The almost silent approach, the sudden rush past - many people cycle on the pavement these days - can send a puppy skittering away from his owner. Avoid reassuring him or picking him up as this will reinforce his fear. Instead show him a bicycle standing still, and then ask the rider to cycle away slowly, praise and reward the puppy throughout if he is calm, and he learns that this is not something that harms him.

Puppies and dogs are exercised in parks, open spaces and on beaches. Children will be present at all of these, so one of the main priorities is to introduce the puppy to children. This is easy if there are children in the house, but where there are not, owners need to seek out families with children, and ask the parents' permission to introduce them to the puppy. Try to avoid children you know to be very noisy or excitable at this stage - the approach needs to be calm, not a boisterous rush at the puppy who is likely to duck away in panic. A frightening experience makes a lasting impression - more about that later.

Take time to introduce him to other animals and ensure from the start that he is taught they are not for chasing. It's worth driving out into the country if you live in town so that he sees sheep, cattle, horses, as well as the more familiar cats and birds that abound in town and country. He should be on lead while near livestock. The opportunity to chase should never be given, and the farmer has the right to shoot a dog he believes to be pestering livestock. Similarly if you live in the country, it's worth ensuring the puppy is taken into town where he will experience plenty of people, traffic and movement.

All of these introductions take place after the puppy goes out into the world, but of course there is much that can be done in the weeks prior to the completion of his vaccination programme. In fact it is vital that the puppy does not lead a wholly secluded life in the weeks between leaving the litter and going outside the house at twelve or thirteen weeks. Many opportunities for valuable lessons will have been lost. In these early weeks ask friends and neighbours to call as frequently as possible. Ask them to sit down, provide them with several treats, and allow the puppy to approach them in his own time. Many a puppy has been frightened badly by well meaning visitors who dive at him exclaiming how lovely he is. Small wonder he takes refuge behind the sofa or your legs! Picking the puppy up and handing him to a visitor is a negative experience. Instead allow the puppy to approach when he is ready, even if this is several minutes after their arrival. Some puppies will rush to greet visitors of course; every puppy is different.

Even the youngest puppy can be taken out in the car. His first experience of car riding is likely to have been the time at which you collected him from his breeder. His second ride may well be to visit the vet. Neither of these will have happy connotations, so the next introduction should be one which will bring pleasure to the puppy. Probably the easiest way is to put the puppy in the car and feed him one of his meals while the car remains stationary. On the next occasion it can be driven with the puppy secure in the back of the car. No puppy should be in the front seat or, even worse, sitting on the driver's lap. If you are forced to brake sharply he could be catapulted through the windscreen or even against the back of your head. If the car is a saloon there is a safety harness available which can be attached to the rear seat belts and make travel safe for both puppy and driver. An estate or hatchback can be fitted with a dog guard, or his crate can be erected in the back, again protecting both puppy and driver.

It can be very difficult to behave calmly when a large dog approaches a very small puppy. Our instinct may be to pick up the puppy or shout at the large dog. Both store up problems for the future. Puppies need to learn greeting rituals with other dogs. Very few dogs will attack a puppy. Being overprotective and pulling the puppy away leads to aggression. Some older dogs will roll the puppy over to put him in his place if he is too enthusiastic in his greeting. This is a valuable lesson and it is not an attack. Dogs will sniff the puppy's mouth and genital area, and the puppy will almost certainly do the same to the older dog. Keeping the lead loose, and allowing these normal investigations to take place will pay dividends when the puppy meets the next dog, and the next, and all the others he will encounter throughout his life.

Last, but far from least in the arsenal of socialisation opportunities available to the owner, are puppy socialisation classes. These first appeared in the 1990's and rapidly grew in popularity. They should not be confused with beginner obedience classes where the puppies will be older. Socialisation classes usually begin as soon as the puppy has completed his vaccination programme, and these special classes usually run for six to eight weeks. The whole family is encouraged to attend, and the classes are kept small so that each puppy feels unthreatened and there is time for the instructor to give individual help and advice. Basic obedience exercises are taught using rewards, and the puppies are able to play and mix with others of their own age in a safe environment. This early mixing and training is invaluable, and the confidence it gives the puppy is well worth the time spent.

Socialisation is a few short weeks of intense concentrated exposure to many people, places and situations. It may sound like hard work, but it takes place in such a short space of time and the benefits of having a puppy that is confident, outgoing, well balanced and able to cope with whatever life throws at him far outweigh the time and effort needed. Training of the puppy will of course continue long after these initial weeks, and may include taking him to classes for some months, or even years if the owner gets hooked on obedience training!

Make yourself a plan, take account of your lifestyle, and introduce your puppy to as many people, places and situations as you can manage. Remember it is not enough for him to meet one baby, one child, one teenager, one man, and so on. Repeated exposures to people and places will pay dividends. The old adage "you get out what you put in" is never more true than when planning socialisation.

COPING WITH A FEAR RESPONSE

At some time the puppy will meet something or someone who frightens him. It may be the sudden appearance of the window cleaner at the window, the mail falling on top of him as he sleeps in the hall, the rattle of a ladder, a bicycle racing by, a child approaching very quickly, perhaps patting the puppy hard on his head, a larger dog rushing up off lead, a car back firing, an umbrella being opened right next to his head, a carrier bag flapping in the wind.......any one of a thousand things that you and I take for granted may cause a fear response. So what to do?

Avoid the very human response of picking the puppy up, cuddling him, and murmuring comforting words. Natural as it may be, this is not a canine response, and you will effectively reinforce the behaviour. The puppy will be convinced that there is something to fear. Instead, ignore the fearful response, remove him from the situation causing the fear, and ensure that next time he meets a similar situation it is positive and pleasant for him.

There are any number of things which may cause a fearful response. The world is after all a very new place to a young puppy. However well you plan, there will always be the unexpected that catches you unawares. Just remember the golden rule of ignoring the fearful response, and then put the puppy into a situation where he can be praised. It can be something as simple as moving away a few feet, asking for a sit, and praising and rewarding him. Then you take every opportunity at home and outdoors to clatter saucepans, rattle things, and shake plastic bags until those fearsome things become commonplace.

USING REWARDS

What is a reward? Rewards have been mentioned several times and so the question "What is a reward?" may seem an unnecessary one. But what we see as reward and what the dog sees as reward are rather different. The obvious rewards are food, toys, praise, touch, attention, a good run, games and playing together. These are all powerful rewards, and you will soon learn what your puppy sees as the best reward. For most puppies it will be food - never underestimate the power of food. Food equals survival, and all living things are programmed to survive.

But you may find you have a puppy who revels in a game, loves a few moments of tugging on a toy with you or has a favourite toy which he will enjoy holding or carrying for a moment or two. That's fine - use what works. Touch is important to a puppy - they are born with a sense of touch and take great comfort from their mother licking and nosing them even before they can see her. You will find your puppy loves to be stroked, long gentle strokes are soothing and pleasurable. You may find he responds to praise - and praise should always be given. We may be in a situation where we have no toy and no food when our puppy does something deserving reward. Use any of these, or a combination of them - keep the puppy's interest.

Initially reward every response to a cue you give, and throw in an occasional surprise reward when the puppy does something without a cue. For instance, you may find that if you are teaching him to sit before his food bowl is put down, after a few days he will sit when he sees the bowl in your hand. Praise and reward him well for he has just shown you he has learnt what you want.

Once he responds reliably to a cue, then you begin to reduce rewards so that you speed up response. If you keep up rewards for every response for too long, he will begin to react more slowly or he may only respond when he sees a reward is available. So you begin to reward for the quickest and the best responses. Even while offering reduced rewards, remember that all-important praise, even if you shorten it to a simple "yes" to tell him he has done the right thing.

HOUSE RULES - OR SETTING BOUNDARIES

It's sensible to decide early on, preferably even before your puppy joins your household, just what is and is not acceptable behaviour. Keep in mind that as young as five weeks old the puppy's brain is very similar to that of an adult dog. In other words, the puppy is able to learn. So when your puppy joins you at the age of eight weeks, gentle training of those essential basics can start immediately.

For many years owners were advised to ensure that they used a series of rules which were drawn up by taking account of how a wolf pack is structured. The leading wolves, sometimes termed "alpha" but more recently termed "breeders", choose the sleeping place, guard the opening to the den, have first pick of any available food, and decide the route the pack follows. All other animals in the pack defer to them, always allowing the leading pair the right of decision.

It's easy to see how these were translated into a series of rules which suggested that a dog allowed to sleep in the bedroom or on the bed made him our equal. Allowing him to push through doorways or lead the way downstairs was said to raise his status. Stroke him when he comes to you for attention and he has taken control. Ensure you eat before you feed the puppy, or he may believe he is top of the pack; remember the leading wolves have first pickings of available food.

But the reality is rather different. Research in the late 1990s, and continuing to the present day, shows that the dogs that live with us are indeed descendants of the wolf. DNA testing has proved that conclusively. But.....it also seems probable that our dogs descend from semi-solitary wolves who scavenged around the camps of man, and who were less fearful and were willing to eat in sight of man. Through natural selection over a period of time, the dog that evolved was smaller, with a smaller brain, more suited to the life of a scavenger than a hunter.

Thus we are living with a dog that is not a direct descendent of a pack animal. It follows that if we try to behave as "pack leader" it has no meaning for the dog, and serves only to confuse. We are after all two different species, and as such we are not members of the same pack. Of course, we can mimic "pack rules" to some extent. We can feed the dog after we have eaten, stop him going downstairs ahead of us, never allow him to instigate a game, or come to us for a cuddle, even take over his bed from time to time. But what we cannot do is give the facial, body, tail and sound signals that the lead wolf or dog would give if a lesser member of the pack stepped out of line. In short, we cannot behave like a dog any more than a dog can behave like a human.

Dogs, like all living things, are programmed to survive. And to survive they need food, shelter, warmth, company, the opportunity to meet a mate and produce the next generation. As we, the humans, provide the food our dogs need, choose what and when they eat, when they are exercised, groomed, when they are played with, where they sleep, and whether or not they are allowed to breed, we already control all those fundamental needs. Our dogs, opportunists though they are, do not spend their days planning to take over the world, or even our household. Equally, there is no need for us to constantly prove our superiority. Our role is to be a responsible owner who socialises and trains our dogs to live with us. We guide and train him in acceptable behaviour, and at the same time try to understand his needs and natural behaviours. There you have the recipe for living in peace with your puppy, and the dog that he will become.

Choose the boundaries you want to set for your puppy, teach them and be consistent. He will quickly learn what is and what is not acceptable. Interaction with your puppy and with the dog he grows into is important, and it builds a wonderful relationship between you.

So, if you are happy to have your puppy sleep in your bedroom, there is no reason not to allow him to do so.

If you like him on the sofa with you as you relax, that's fine. Teach him to come up on cue, and teach him to come down off the sofa on cue, reward him for complying, and you have harmony.

Play tug of war games if you want to. Tugging is a great energy burner, and a lot of fun. Teach a release cue "give" or "off", ensure that sometimes you win the game and that sometimes the dog wins. If he never wins, he will cease to play and a great training tool is lost.

Teach him to wait at the top of the stairs for safety reasons, but surprise him sometimes and send him down ahead of you.

If it suits you to feed him as you get breakfast and again as you are preparing supper, then do so. Teach him that food comes in his bowl, but that it never comes from your plate or from the table - you will never then be pestered for food.

If you never want him on the sofa then never let him join you there. If you do not want him in your bedroom, then as soon as he is house-trained (remember those night time needs!) move his bed or crate out of your bedroom. If you do not want him upstairs at all, then teach him that the stairs are out of bounds. Use a baby gate initially if necessary until he understands where he is or is not allowed to go.

When he comes to you for a stroke or to invite a game, then either play with him, or give him a moment's attention, and then give the cue to "settle down". This cue will quickly come to mean he can play by himself if he wants to, but that you are not going to at that moment. You call him to you for praise, a stroke, or a game - why then should it be wrong for him to approach you?

THINK ABOUT THOSE EVERYDAY SITUATIONS

Puppy socialisation classes and higher level training classes will teach you to handle your puppy in a kind and fair way, using rewards to tell him that he is responding as you want him to. But keep in mind that whether you are training your puppy in class or at home in the house or garden, you are training him in just one situation and that situation is actually often an artificial one.

In class all the puppies will be on lead or off lead at controlled times. Owners will be very focussed on their puppy. Other owners and children in the class will be encouraged to approach him gently, rewarding him as they do so. But outside in the real world, he is going to meet very different situations. In the park there will be dogs off lead, and some of them will not be under control - a strange dog may well rush at yours, barking loudly. A car may hoot just as it passes as you wait to cross the road, or a lorry release its air brakes adjacent to you. A cyclist may come racing past, just missing your puppy as he does so. He may be responding really well at home and in class, but you will almost certainly find that his response in a different place will be less reliable, and sometimes non-existent.

So here we are going to consider "situational training" or "lessons for life". That is training that takes place in a real life situation rather than a controlled one such as in class. You will already have visited some of the areas during his socialisation period. In that time you were concentrating on ensuring he was exposed to as many different people, places and experiences as you could manage, while at the same time ensuring he was not frightened or overwhelmed. Now you will be building on those early experiences and training him to respond to your cues in many different situations. For example, achieving a recall when you call your puppy at home is a success, but it is very different when you are recalling him in the park where there are numerous distractions in the shape of interesting smells, people, and of course other dogs. Even in the controlled confines of a class you may find that he runs across the greet another dog rather than return to you when he is called.

So, now you begin working to ensure that he responds to you whatever the distraction, and wherever you both may be. It's important when you begin this "training for life" that you do not overwhelm the puppy. Time is now on your side - there is not the urgent need for introducing him to many different situations as in the socialisation period. You can of course begin to train him in different places as soon as his vaccinations are complete, but it is probably better to concentrate on socialisation and puppy classes in that period. What you learn about your puppy in those weeks will be useful knowledge as you begin to extend his training into other areas of your life.

And there is a key phrase - the areas of your life. It's well worth sitting down - much as you did when planning his socialisation - and making a list of all those places you go or want to go which will also involve your puppy. Some of your training will be done with just you and your puppy. But if you have friends with dogs - preferably ones that are trained to come when called, sit at the kerb, and walk on the lead without pulling - then enlist their help so that you have a ready made distraction at hand some of the time. This has the added bonus too that the more your puppy mixes with other dogs, the more adept he will become at communicating with his own kind.

What might you consider here? You might meet with dog owning friends and their dogs at the country park or the woods, the shopping precinct, the railway or bus station, or near one of several local schools, close to a busy main road where traffic is thundering past or on the bridge which crosses both a motorway and a railway. You are now a dog owner, so you take no notice of the weather. Dog owners walk in all weathers so it may be a lovely sunny day, or it may be a cold one and it may well be raining. It's real life, so no point in waiting on the weather!

This has the added bonus that your puppy sees you and passers-by wearing a variety of clothing - hats, top coats, boots and umbrellas as well as lighter clothes when the weather is kind. They will encounter bicycles whisking past them on the pavements, the odd motorcycle on the pavement has not been unknown, and then there is the occasional car door which is thrust open just as you are walking by. In each of these situations you want your puppy to remain calm, and to sit or down - whichever you choose to cue.

You might stand near the school as the children come out. The noise of several hundred excited children released at the same time from the confines of the classroom has to be experienced to be believed. Here again you want your puppy to be calm, and to respond to whatever cue you give. You might join friends and their dogs, and sit on the seats in the shopping precinct, settle the dogs and just sit and watch the world go by for a while - who said it was all hard work? Walk home just as the streams of children leave the school, and walk through the precinct many times where your puppy will encounter different people, shopping trolleys, bags and baskets, children on roller blades and cycles, perhaps meet someone with a wheelchair or just walking with a stick. Talk to your friends by all means for here you are enacting real life. But equally keep an eye on your puppy - note any problems or places where he is uneasy - and work on those in the coming weeks.

Perhaps you can arrange to meet a friend with a dog and take a bus to town - few buses will take more than two dogs at a time. If you are likely to take country holidays, it's worth driving out with a friend or two with dogs and walk them adjacent to fields with horses, sheep and cattle. Your puppy's life may depend on you teaching him that these animals are not for chasing. You will see the dogs become very relaxed with one another, but make sure that not all your training is done with other dogs, or you may find your own begins to depend on their presence.

Training for life needs to cover as many combinations of experiences as possible. When your dog will sit and wait on cue while other dogs are rushing around, then you have a real breakthrough. A really important part of training for life is to ensure that your puppy or dog comes back to you no matter what. If you can visit a park or country park with friends with dogs, once in the country park a completely different situation pertains. Here the dogs can play with each other, with other dogs, and of course, with you. Perish the thought that you will walk along chatting busily with friends while your dogs cavort out of sight and out of mind. Your puppy will become more relaxed and learn to respond sociably to an unknown dog if one approaches. Here you can practise recalls many, many times in the safety of the park and with all those wonderful distractions. The more recalls you practise and the more different locations and distractions you work with, the better his response will be.

Training in the park, alone with your puppy or with friends with their dogs provides such a variety - squirrels, rabbits and inevitably their droppings, joggers, picnickers, kites flying, as well as the occasional golfer practising his shots who sends a ball whistling past. All of these activities provide splendid opportunities for you to distract him from whatever he is doing and call him in, rewarding him suitably when he arrives. Don't let your puppy or dog learn that coming back to you means the lead goes on immediately, and he is marched off home. There's no pleasure in that.

Every recall should be fun and rewarding, and when that last call comes and it is time to go, he will come to you because he has no unpleasant associations with so doing. You will see many times a scenario where an owner calls his dog, the dog ignores him, and when he eventually returns he is shouted at or even slapped. If your recall fails at some time - and it may well - then smile, reward and praise the return no matter how long it takes. If you punish a slow return, then the next will be slower, and the one after that may not happen at all.

If you and your family enjoy a visit to the pub in the evening, then take the puppy along. Some will not welcome a dog inside of course, but most will accept a dog in the gardens. Have a snack or a meal there, but no titbits here for the puppy other than his reward for settling down on cue. If you visit the seaside regularly, take the puppy along and let him get used to the sound of waves, the shriek of gulls, and the feeling of sand or shingle beneath his feet. Encourage him into the shallows, and let him paddle. Later you may want to encourage him to swim - dogs are natural swimmers and it is great exercise. Sadly dogs are less popular than they used to be - many open spaces, beaches and public places are now banned to us. A dog that can be taken into any situation in which you know that he will behave acceptably, and who will return to you no matter what the distraction, is a joy to own and a nuisance to no one.

TEACHING YOUR PUPPY THOSE BASIC CUES

What follows is a brief description of two kind and gentle ways to teach your puppy those all important basic cues. There are of course many more things you will teach him, but installing a reliable "come", "sit" and "down" can be done in those very early weeks when the puppy first joins you, and continued once he is out and about following completion of his vaccination programme. The first method described - lure and reward - has been in use for some years, while the second - Clicker training - came into popular use in the mid 1990s. Both are successful and gentle ways of teaching your puppy, so it is a question of you deciding which you find works for you both.

There are other methods, and unfortunately you will still find advocates of putting a choke chain on your dog, even on a puppy, and yanking him to bring him to heel, pushing him into a sit with your hand on his lower back, and pulling his legs forward to bring him into a down. There is no denying that these harsher methods will teach the puppy to respond to the given cues, but these forceful methods also instil fear and distrust. Just think what a dog learns if every time another dog comes into view, he is jerked on a choke chain and hears a shouted "LEAVE". Within a very short space of time that dog will begin to be aggressive or fearful in the presence of other dogs. Whatever the situation, try always to think what the end result might be.

Reward training relies on the owner teaching a word (cue) to which the puppy responds, and for which initially he is rewarded every time he responds. It means that the owner needs to use a happy relaxed tone of voice, and to use the same word every time. Sounds easy, but when there are several people in the household quite often different words are used for the same required response, eg "here" and "come" - very confusing for the puppy. Reward training works, and many owners will be happy to use this method.

Clicker training also works on the principle of rewarding the dog, but initially no cues are given at all. You will find a more detailed explanation in one of several books devoted solely to clicker and the many things you can teach using this kind and gentle method. Briefly the difference lies in the fact that no cues are given initially - you let the clicker do the talking. The puppy is lured into the wanted position, and instead of being praised and rewarded, he receives a click and treat. The click serves to tell him this is what is wanted. It is a single clear sound, with no emphasis on tone of voice or use of a specific word. Later, a cue is added, at which time the sequence changes. You then give a cue, the puppy responds, then you click and treat, finally phasing out the click altogether. Think of the clicker simply as a tool to help you communicate in a definite and unambiguous way. If that sounds complicated, I promise it is much easier to do than it is to describe!

Clicker training has an additional bonus in that you do not have to wait until your puppy or dog has given the whole wanted action before he is clicked and treated. The clicker allows you to shape a wanted response by rewarding any movement towards the end product - this is something you cannot do with reward training. As an example - if you are teaching a down, hold the food in your hand and take it down between the puppy's paws. If his head goes down, click and treat; if he bends at the elbow, click and treat; if he begins to lower his hindquarters, click and treat; if his forelegs go down onto the ground, click and treat. When the whole body goes down, click and now is the time to give four or five treats.

Many owners using clicker do find that once their puppy understands that click equals reward, he begins to offer all sorts of different actions. It makes it possible to teach many different responses, from serious to fun. If you already have an older dog that was taught by reward methods, you can still teach him using a clicker - often you will find the dog takes to it with amazing ease. As an example, among many other things, my young bitch has been taught to bow - she sits, puts one leg forward and dips her head - it's very beguiling and she uses it to good effect with visitors!

Gentle training, using rewards, strengthens the bond between you and your puppy. Try several short training sessions each day, making it part and parcel of the time you spend together. Don't be afraid to experiment to find which method works best for you both. Your puppy will "catch on" to some actions more quickly than others.

SETTLE DOWN

Before moving on to discuss which of the two methods you might decide to use, a very useful cue to teach is "settle down". It has a multitude of uses from preventing the puppy pestering while you are eating, to telling him in a gentle way that you do not want to play if he brings a toy. You can cheat a little here by watching to see when the puppy is going to settle down of his own accord, give the cue, praise him and toss some small rewards. It is unfair to expect the puppy, or a dog, to lay down and sleep for hours simply because we are busy with other things.

TEACHING USING THE LURE AND REWARD METHOD

COME:

This cue is given first as this is probably the most important cue you will ever teach your puppy. Young puppies are usually very ready to follow us and we can use this to good advantage. Try to ensure that you have a good recall prior to the puppy reaching the age of around eighteen weeks. This is the time when that biddable little puppy begins to feel more independent, and when he may begin to be deaf to calls.

Initially only use "come" when the puppy is approaching you, bend down or tap your knee, say his name and "come" in a happy tone. If he is wearing a collar slip your finger in his collar, praise and reward him immediately. Then let him go to play again.

When you are about to feed him, call his name (if he is not already waiting close to you!), and as he approaches give the cue. Reward him with his dinner bowl.

If you are certain the puppy knows his name, then hold a food reward in front of his nose, say his name and "come", step back, and as he comes to you slip your fingers in his collar, reward and praise.

Initially you will reward your puppy or dog every time he responds. As his response becomes more reliable, you can reduce the rewards to encourage him to work harder for his treat. Give a reward on the second recall, next time on the first, another time on the third - keep him guessing. The reason for changing the frequency of rewards is explained earlier in "Using Rewards".

Teaching a recall in this way will work equally well with an older dog, perhaps a rescued one, that has not previously been taught to come.

SIT:
Keep in mind that if the puppy's head goes up, his back end goes down and you can see how easy it is to lure him into a sit with no need to press on his lower back.

Hold a small food reward in your hand, let the puppy see it, then take your hand slowly back so that it is above his eye line. As he looks up to see the treat, his bottom will go down. Give the cue "sit". Reward and praise him as he complies. Repeat this as often as you can while the puppy is interested and responsive - short lessons work best with puppies as their attention span is short and they tire.

Some puppies may shuffle backwards to try to see the treat in your hand. You may need to experiment to see just where you need to hold your hand to elicit the desired response. If all else fails, have the puppy close to a wall or corner so that he cannot shuffle backwards.

Initially reward him each and every time he complies with the lure and cue to sit. You will need to experiment to see when he begins to respond just to the cue alone without the need to use a lure. Once that happens, you can begin to reduce the reward to intermittent as in teaching the recall.

DOWN:
Sit on the floor (it does save backache!) with some treats. Encourage the puppy to sit, using a food lure if necessary, then take your hand with the reward down to the floor between his front paws and slightly forward. As he goes down, give the cue "down" reward and praise. Repeat several times - beware of boring the puppy. Change to something else if his attention starts to wander. Most puppies will go down very easily, but you always get the occasional one who can do a near handstand - front paws go down while his bottom stays up in the air.

So try a different tack. Sit on the floor, raise one leg so that it makes an arch, lure the puppy under the arch of your leg so that he has to go down to get the food reward.

USING CLICKER TRAINING

A different method by which to teach those basic cues:

COME: (Clicker method)
First you need to teach the puppy what the click actually means. Press the clicker, and when he looks up, reward him with a tiny but tasty treat. No words are used initially. Once the puppy understands that the sound is followed by a reward, you can begin to teach him many different responses. If you wish, you can wait for the puppy to perform the action you want to teach, then click and reward him. This can be time consuming, so most of us do lure the puppy into the required position. But as time goes by, you may see things you really like, so never miss the opportunity to click and reward something you want. Keep in mind that adding in a cue comes later.

The principle is similar to reward training. As the puppy starts to come towards you, call his name and show him the treat. As he reaches you, slip your hand in his collar, click and treat. At this stage you do NOT use the word "come" or praise him. The click tells him he has done what is wanted, the food rewards him. So the sequence here is name, response, click, treat.

Over the day, and the following days repeat this as many times as you are able. The number of repetitions necessary varies considerably from dog to dog - some understand very quickly, others take longer. Be patient. Once the puppy is reliably coming to you, then it is time to put in the cue "come". So now the sequence will be cue, response, click, treat. There is no hurry to put a cue in - be really sure that the puppy is reliably offering the behaviour, whether it is "come" or any other cue. Here again you will initially reward every single response, but will reduce this to intermittent as described in "Using Rewards".

SIT: (Clicker method)
When you use a clicker you can wait for a behaviour to happen and click and reward it, or you can lure it. The information below indicates using a lure

First day at home

Watching you, watching me

Getting to know you

Crackers!

A little assistance in the garden

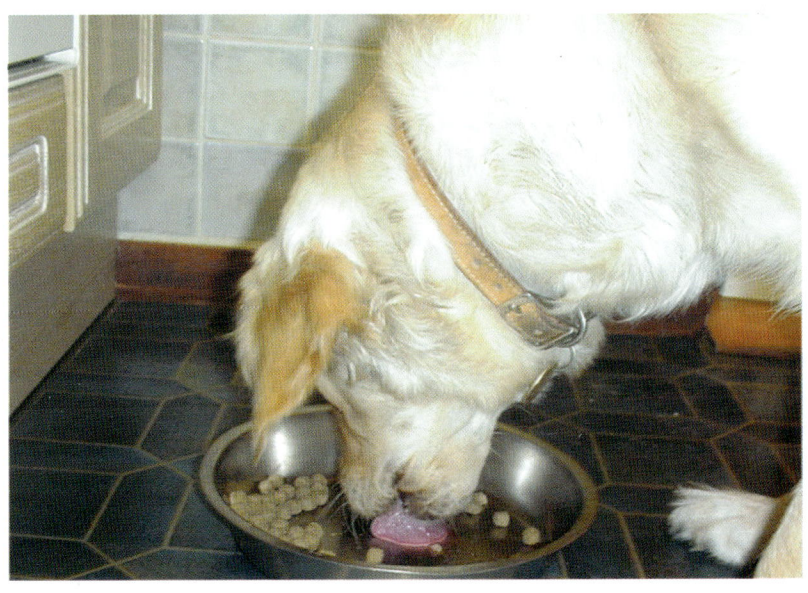

The best time of day

Not ALWAYS an angel!

Good companions

because with a young puppy you may find this easier than waiting for him to do something you want to teach. But the choice is yours.

Have available a dozen or so small food rewards and the clicker. Lure the puppy into a sit by holding the food just above his eye line and moving your hand back. As his bottom hits the floor, click and reward him. Repeat this while the puppy is interested, keeping in mind that puppies have shorter attention spans than older dogs, and they tire much more quickly.

Here again, there is no hurry to put in a cue. When your puppy is coming to you and sitting on arrival, or begins to offer you a sit when he sees the clicker in your hand, then is the time to add in the verbal "Sit".

Rewards at first will be for every sit, but as the puppy begins to understand what is wanted, then they can become intermittent.

DOWN: (Clicker method)
Sit on the floor with the clicker in your hand and some food treats in your pocket. Lure the puppy into the down in the same way as in reward training, but as he goes down click and reward. No verbal cue is used at this stage. Repeat the lure into the down as many times as you can while the puppy is interested.

Here again, there is no hurry to put in a cue. When your puppy goes down of his own accord, then is the time to add in the verbal "Down".

Rewards at first will be for every down, but as the puppy begins to understand what is wanted, then they can become intermittent. Remember reducing reward increases the response, so reward the best and fastest responses to keep him interested.

What you may well find with using a clicker is that once the puppy recognises that something he does brings the click, and subsequently a reward, he will begin to offer you those behaviours he has learnt bring him reward. So you may see him go into a sit even though you were about to work on a down. In the early stages, don't miss an opportunity to click and reward him. Then wait and see if he then goes into a down, and again you have the opportunity to click and reward him.

Owners are often surprised by how quickly a puppy begins to offer different actions in the hope of that reward. (If you decide to try clicker training with an older dog previously trained by lure and reward, you will find he too will begin to experiment to see what brings reward). If you see something you like, then click and reward it. Always keep in mind that if an action is rewarded it will be repeated. If you miss it once it won't matter, but keep ignoring it and the puppy will cease to offer it.

CANINE COMMUNICATION

Dogs communicate with other dogs in one of three ways: sound, scent, and body/facial signals. While we can learn to understand both sound and body/facial signals, the messages transmitted by scent remain a mystery to us. Given the sensitivity of the dog's ability to scent, this method of communication is an important one for him.

Learning to read the signals your puppy gives is fun, and you will learn much from just watching him interact with you, with children, with other dogs, and of course with the world around him.

During a meeting of two or more dogs, they will briefly sniff each other's mouths, and then move to sniff each other's anal and genital areas. An enormous amount of information is gleaned from this - the sex, sexual condition, health, and whether or not the dog or bitch is neutered is all apparent to the dog. Urine is a transmitter of much information. Every owner of male dogs will be aware of the numerous times the dog "cocks his leg" while out on a walk. A male dog will often be seen to urinate over the earlier marking of another dog, and some perform extraordinary acrobatic feats to ensure their urine goes higher and further than that of previous dogs. Some scratch their back feet vigorously as if to make sure that the scent travels far and wide. From this we may deduce that not only does urine convey health messages, it also conveys the strength and power of the dog.

Bitches also read the urine markings of dogs that have been there earlier, but are less likely to add their own. Like the male dog, their urine also carries chemical messages called pheromones which contain much information. While she is in season, the bitch's urine will convey a potent message to every male dog. The dog may become very active and excited, and begin tracking industriously to find the bitch who has left such an attractive message. Should the two meet then a mating resulting in a litter of puppies is virtually inevitable.

Faeces also convey messages to the passing dog. The anal glands which lie at each side of the anus secrete a substance as the dog empties his bowel. The exact purpose of these glands is not really known, other than that the secretions carry pheromones which provide all the essential information outlined in the above paragraphs. Dogs may also involuntarily empty their anal glands when they are in a state of great fear.

Saliva too contains these chemical messages. The mother of newly born puppies licks them to put her scent on them, which will then lead them to her milk supply. Often when dogs meet they will sniff and lick each other's mouths, and will learn something of the other dog's health and condition, as well as whether or not he has eaten recently.

To us the most obvious method of communication is sound. But for dogs this is less powerful than scent and visual signals. They are however able to produce a range of sounds - bark, growl, howl, yelp, whine, whimper, moan - and within each of these they are able to produce different tones. You will quickly recognise the difference between a "come and play" bark and one with which your dog seeks to warn you that there is a stranger approaching. You will also quickly register the yelp that occurs if you step back unwarily and the puppy is underfoot! There are a range of growls too, from a light toned growling which you may hear when you are playing a tugging game with your puppy, to a grumbling "leave me alone", and on up the scale.

It's easy to be fooled about what is being "said" if you concentrate on only one part of the dog. The whole body tells the story, and our dogs show their mood and emotions very clearly if we take time to learn. Signals are often very subtle, flowing quickly from one to another. Watch the eyes, how the ears are held, the position of the tail - a wagging tail is not always friendly! - if there are hackles showing over the neck of the dog or his rump.

Is the body tense or relaxed? Is the facial expression relaxed, or are the eyes staring? Is the dog standing tall and leaning forward?

A tail tucked down between the legs is a clear indicator that the dog is worried or frightened, but one held stiffly with the hair bristling tells a whole different story.

Facial expressions are very subtle too. A bold confident dog looks directly at another or at a person, while a dog that is anxious glances away, and may even turn his head and shoulder away in a clear message that he is no threat. The nervous one who licks his lips is showing his apprehension.

Even the mouth and tongue tell a story. A slightly open mouth with tongue showing is a relaxed dog comfortable with what is happening around him. But one with open mouth, lips retracted showing maximum teeth is issuing a clear warning. There are many intermediate signals between these two ends of the scale which if you watch interactions frequently, you will soon come to recognise.

And then there is the unmistakable invitation to play. The dog's front end is down on the ground with his back end in the air, tail up, ears up, wide mouth with tongue showing. This is the classic play bow, often accompanied by little barks and pounces as the dog tries to inveigle another dog or a member of his human family to play.

If we watch we will become aware that dogs communicate on three levels - first their emotional response to situations, secondly their social standing, and lastly their needs. They can tell us when they are content, frightened, stressed, angry, or in pain. It takes time and concentration to learn to read them easily and quickly, but it pays dividends in cementing the bond between us.

It's easy to think that they know just a few basic cues, but the fact is that our dogs can and do learn many words, and may well respond to upwards of a hundred different cues if they are taught kindly and with reward. Our dogs spend much time watching us and learning what our body language means. Through their observations of us, they quickly learn the pattern of our days, even to the point of recognising when the time for food is fast approaching, or that we are wearing clothing that almost certainly means an outing for them. It seems a fair exchange that we do our best to understand what their language means. The end result is a richer and more satisfying relationship with the puppy and the dog that he will become.

MORE THAN JUST A GAME

Play is important throughout the life of your puppy. Within their litter puppies begin to play as early as three to four weeks old. These games have their serious side, for while they play, the puppies are learning all the skills they need to be dogs. Their muscles are developing, their brain is developing, and they are learning to coordinate their movement. The games they play teach them to inhibit their bite; bite a litter mate too hard and play ceases - a valuable life lesson. Their mother will also play with them, teaching them how to hunt, to pounce, and to shake their prey. Once they become ours of course, their prey will be toys - and probably the odd slipper or two. But in those vital weeks with their mother and litter mates play and interaction between them teaches many skills and gives them the ability to cope with problems and resolve them.

We spoke earlier of the importance of the breeder providing some early socialisation, and now the puppy has passed into your hands, you can do much to enhance the bond with the new puppy through play. Play makes him part of our social group, and provides him with essential mental and physical stimulation which he would of course receive if he continued to live with other dogs. As he grows from puppy to juvenile, and then on to adult, the duration and kind of games change to take account of his growing size and strength.

All puppies will enjoy playing with toys, and there is a vast array available in the stores. Opt for safe toys - just that bit too large for there to be any possibility of him swallowing them. Soft toys are fine, but check that eyes, ears, and tails are safely fixed. Puppies will chase and pounce on a rolled toy or a tossed ball, and it is never too soon to start the basics of a retrieve. Dogs can be given good exercise by teaching them to chase and return with a ball, a Kong or other safe toy.

Remember that your puppy is a natural predator - his instinct will tell him to hunt, so incorporate hunting games into your play sessions and you have found the way to getting and keeping his attention. As he grows, hiding toys and small food treats for him to find will be popular, and again allows him to use instinctive behaviour.

Buy one or two hollow toys, and pop some of his food inside so that he can work to extract the food - far more satisfying than just eating everything from a bowl! If he is fed on a dry complete food, try scattering it on the floor or on the patio sometimes, and let him forage for it.

Training does not have to be a boring time for you and your puppy. Incorporate training into his daily exercise, intersperse it with games, and this all becomes part of his enjoyable interactions with you. As he grows, consider adding in some jumping and perhaps even joining an agility class - good exercise for you both!

Play is more than just a game. Play remains important throughout your puppy's life. Play keeps muscles and organs in good condition, and in addition, it keeps the mind active. Much research has been carried out into the effects of mental and physical stimulation. The conclusions show clearly that the dog that is encouraged to use his brain and who leads an active life suffers less mental deterioration as he ages. Effectively, by playing games, encouraging him to run, chase, catch toys, and join in all the activities that we can devise, we help maintain good health and ensure that he lives the longest life possible.

Have fun!

PREVENTING PUPPY PROBLEMS

PART TWO: COPING WITH COMMON PROBLEMS

PULLING ON THE LEAD

Probably the behaviour which causes most confrontation between dog and owner is pulling on the lead. It's uncomfortable, and it can look very undignified if you are being hauled down the road by an enthusiastically pulling puppy. Keep in mind that by six months old, a puppy of a large breed may weigh 25 kgs or more and have considerable pulling power. In addition the puppy is likely to be panting or coughing as he leans hard into his collar. So early lead training is a must, and you can of course begin at home and in the garden well before he is able to go out into the world.

Arm yourself with a pocketful of small tasty treats. Choose something really special such as tiny slivers of cheese, hot dog, or baked liver. You are about to become the most interesting person in the world to be with. Choose a time when the puppy is hungry - if he is full of food he will be less interested in your rewards - and start his training in the garden where there are few distractions.

Attach his lead, preferably a long lead. Take just one step forward and then give the cue "Sit". Praise and give him a small food treat. Take several steps, cue "Sit", praise and reward. Do this several times a day for three or four days. Nothing more; be content with those few steps.

Clip on the lead again and this time walk forward and keep walking, praise and reward every few steps while the lead remains loose. If he pulls, stop, say nothing and give no reward. Step off again, and reward for the loose lead. If he persists in trying to pull, change direction quickly, praising and rewarding, or clicking and rewarding when he turns and follows you. Take care not to jerk or pull on the lead. Keep your movements as smooth as possible.

Once he is paying attention and the lead is loose most of the time, then progress to outside of the garden, using the same techniques. Your puppy will soon learn that walking with you is fun and rewarding, but pulling means you stop, ignore him and he receives no reward. It's useful to teach a cue such as "close", "with me" or "heel". It does not matter if your puppy is not walking strictly at heel. What you want is to be able to walk comfortably without him pulling ahead. Chatting companionably often works well to keep his attention on you, and if he's a puppy that enjoys toys, then a toy held in your other hand can serve to keep his attention.

An alternative is to use a head collar which fits over his face and fastens behind his head. This has an instant effect of preventing pulling. It gives you control and once the puppy has become used to it, it is a valuable tool in many other situations. Some owners prefer to use a head collar as soon as the puppy is being taught to walk on a lead and so avoid him ever learning he can pull. The downside is that some members of the public see a head collar as a muzzle, and do not understand it is simply a collar.

JUMPING UP

Puppies jump up to greet their mother and lick her mouth as they do so. This is normal behaviour, and it is both a greeting and a request for food. Although the breeder introduces semi-solid food and then solid food to the puppies to aid weaning, puppies still retain this instinctive behaviour, and many bitches do help to wean their puppies by regurgitating partly digested food for them. So when our puppies jump up at us, they are transferring this natural behaviour to greet us and ask for food.

Initially a puppy that jumps up to greet us can seem very endearing. How nice that he wants to welcome us! And of course he does want to welcome us, but as he grows and especially when he is wet and muddy, this jumping up can seem rather less attractive. There is of course also the risk that the puppy will knock over a small child or a frail elderly visitor.

Instinctively we may push the puppy off and say "get down" in a sharp tone. But in canine terms what we actually do here is reward the puppy with touch and with attention. Sometimes you may see advice to knee the puppy in the chest as he jumps, but he will be much quicker than you. Additionally, few people want to risk hurting the puppy if a knee actually connects with his body.

Preventing this behaviour is easy, but here you have to be very firm with the whole family. Visitors too need to be asked to respond in the same way, despite the fact they may well say "Oh, I don't mind". If just <u>one</u> person encourages the puppy to jump up, or makes a fuss of him if he manages to do so, then any work you have done to prevent the problem will be undone and you will have to start all over again.

When the puppy jumps up, ignore him. Turn away, fold your arms, do not look at him, and stay silent. The puppy may try again - after all, to date it has got him a cuddle, a stroke, and a "hallo". Initially you may well find the puppy bounces up at you again, and again, and again. You are behaving differently from what he expects, so he will try harder and harder to achieve success. Keep ignoring any jumping up, say nothing, and avoid eye contact.

He <u>will</u> give up! All four feet will go back on the ground, and now you immediately look at him, bend down quickly, praise him, give him a small reward, and stroke him. His response may be to jump up again in excitement. So immediately take your hands away, and ignore him again. Once his feet are on the floor, again praise him warmly and reward him.

Most puppies will make the connection very quickly. Others will try harder and harder to get attention by jumping up. Be consistent, and he will get the message. Feet on floor equals treats and praise - puppy heaven in fact! You can at this point, if you wish, give a cue to "Sit," and then praise and reward. Once sitting, it is impossible for a puppy to jump, and this double approach is usually quickly learned and very successful.

PLAY BITING

Here again this problem stems from puppyhood. While with their litter mates, puppies play some very rough games with each other. They chase, paw each other, mouth, stalk, and leap on each other. This is part of normal development, and this play within the litter teaches them many valuable lessons. One of these is that if you nip or mouth a litter mate too hard, he yelps. If you do it again, you will be shunned by your litter mates. Nobody plays with a bully. In this way the puppies learn to inhibit their bite, and they quickly learn how hard a bite elicits a yelp.

Often this play biting or mouthing continues as the puppy grows. As he gets bigger it hurts more and more, and what an owner may tolerate in an eight week old puppy is much less acceptable in a sixteen week old one. The puppy needs to learn that human skin is tender, and that it is not acceptable to put teeth on it. If it happens any play stops immediately.

Some puppies will respond if you shriek dramatically when teeth meet your skin. You turn away, holding your arm - at this stage some puppies will stop the play biting and come to you gently. But others find you squealing even more exciting and may dash in for another attempt. So here is where ignoring the unwanted comes into its own again.

Do exactly as you did when the puppy was jumping. Ignore him, turn away, and only respond to him when he is calm. At that point you can praise and reward him, stroke him and play if you choose to. If the play biting is very persistent, then as it begins quietly take the puppy outside the room, close the door on him, and ignore him for a few minutes. He will learn from this that play biting ends the game. When you let him back in, greet him pleasantly - the incident is over so recriminations or nagging serve no purpose.

FOOD BOWL TRAINING

One of the behaviours that people find most annoying is when a dog guards his food bowl. This is normal dog behaviour - no dog willingly shares his food with another, but it is unacceptable behaviour to us. So it makes good sense to teach the puppy from day one that people walk by, people approach his bowl, and people touch his bowl. Even young puppies may growl when the bowl is approached, and this can be a dangerous situation if there is a young child or crawling baby in the house.

Each time the puppy is fed, sit down on the floor next to his bowl. Teach him to wait for a few seconds and then give the cue "Take it". Teaching this few seconds delay and permission to eat overcomes many food related problems, such as snatching a biscuit or ice cream from a child's hand.

Keep your hand on the bowl as the puppy is eating. Put your hand right into the bowl talking quietly to the puppy as you do so. Praise him as he eats. Hand feed a few mouthfuls of his food to him, again talking quietly. Stroke his back and head and continue to talk quietly and praise him. Drop into the bowl several small pieces of extra tasty food - chopped chicken, tiny slivers of cheese, chopped meat, even tiny liver tablets which can be purchased at pet stores.

The majority of puppies will quickly accept the presence of their owner near their bowl if this is done, but if yours is one that does not then a slightly different approach usually works wonders. It too teaches the puppy that people near the food bowl are good news. Prepare some extra tasty small pieces of food as above. Give the puppy his normal bowl of food. Now walk past and as you do so throw in two or three pieces of extra tasty food saying "Here you are" or something similar in a cheerful voice. Walk past as many times as possible while he is eating.

Encourage other members of the family including children (under close supervision) to add food to the puppy's bowl in this way. It is sensible to deduct some of his usual food ration while you are carrying out this training process. You may find this works best if you measure out the day's food ration each morning, reduce it by about 10% to allow for plentiful food rewards for this and other training purposes, and set it aside.

In this way you effectively teach him that people bring extra food. They do not take it away - that is an unfair expectation to have of any dog, however young or however old. Once it is put on the floor, it is HIS - you add to it, but you never take away. As soon as the puppy or dog is relaxed and actually welcoming human presence near the bowl - watch for the wag of the tail - he can be stroked down his back and on his neck.

Puppies are initially fed four times a day, reducing to three at twelve weeks, so this gives many opportunities to get this training right. However, if the problem occurs when he is past puppyhood, and he is normally fed only once a day, increase this to twice daily at least for the duration of retraining. Feeding twice a day has the added benefit of maintaining more stable blood sugar levels. This in itself is calming in many dogs.

This method will work equally well in retraining an older puppy or adult dog that has got into the habit of protecting his food. This can become a serious problem with a real risk of aggression, even to the point of the dog chasing people out of the kitchen.

Starting as soon as the puppy joins the household, teaching that few seconds "wait" and letting him realise that people around while he eats are good news is a sure fire way of preventing this problem from ever developing. NEVER take away the bowl just "to prove you can" for you do exactly what the puppy or dog fears - you steal his food, and may well trigger guarding behaviour.

BEGGING AT THE TABLE

This little habit usually starts when someone slips pieces of food to the puppy who is lurking under the table. It may also start with the children sharing their food or crisps with the puppy. Very quickly he begins to demand what was previously given. Puppies can become very vocal if they are used to the family sharing food with them, and it is not forthcoming. Pawing and whining may begin, and the pawing can be quite painful.

To resolve this problem, you have to be prepared to suffer a little. Nothing, absolutely nothing is given to the puppy from the table, or from your plate if you are sitting on the sofa eating from a tray. One solution will be to put the puppy in his crate if he has one, or leave him in the kitchen. Provide him with some suitable chew toys - remember his crate is never used as a punishment. But keep in mind this is prevention rather than cure.

If you choose to crate him while you eat give him a hollow bone or a Kong stuffed with some treats to occupy him. You can even give him his entire meal in this way if you wish. It will both satisfy his hunting instinct and keep him busy.

If you follow the first route you are teaching the puppy that he can no longer expect food to come from the table. The second method is only preventing him from pestering you, but also gives him a reward for settling down elsewhere. Use whichever works best for you and your puppy. You may feel hardhearted at first - puppies are past masters at managing to look as if they are starving!

HOME ALONE

One of the crucial lessons we need to teach our puppy is to cope with being alone. The puppy that is not taught this may well become very stressed, and this may result in him barking constantly, chewing our belongings (and some of the damage can be extensive and expensive), and possibly urinating and defecating indoors in his fear. We may respond angrily when we return, and now the puppy has a double dilemma. He cannot cope alone, but he also learns to fear our return.

Start by leaving him alone for just two or three minutes by closing the door between you. Say nothing, just close the door. Ignore any whining or scratching, and the second he is quiet open the door, praise him and reward him. If you do this every day, several times a day, you can build his tolerance of being alone from just a few minutes to several hours. When you leave the house, leave without any fuss or "be a good boy" departures but greet him cheerfully when you return. If he makes a mistake and there is some damage or he has urinated, ignore it and greet him warmly. You have progressed too quickly. Go back a step or two, and build his confidence again.

Here again is a situation where his crate can be a boon. Of course he should not be left in it for hours on end, but if you are going out for a short time and he is used to his crate, then pop him in, leave him some toys, including suitable ones to chew, and perhaps a Kong with a little food inside.

BARKING

A puppy that barks to alert us is usually encouraged, but one that barks, barks, barks for no apparent reason can become a problem for both owner and neighbours. The puppy's hearing is so much better than ours that he may often respond to sounds which we simply do not hear at all. To prevent barking becoming a problem, we can put it under control by teaching him to bark on cue, and stop on cue.

You can teach the puppy to bark by engaging in such antics as acting as if very excited and exhorting the puppy to "speak", but it is easy to wait until he barks naturally. Then while he is barking, praise him and say "Speak, speak" in an excited tone. The moment he stops, softly give a second cue of "Quiet" and reward him with a treat and plenty of praise. Try to avoid saying "Quiet" while he is actually barking initially as the cue will have no meaning.

After a number of repetitions you should find that the puppy responds to the request for barking and the cue to stop. The way to the puppy's heart is almost always through his stomach, but if yours is one that responds best to a toy and a game, then use that as his reward in this and other training situations.

BARKING IN THE CAR

The puppy or dog that barks in the car can quickly become a nightmare. It can be very distracting, and for some drivers the noise makes them feel quite agitated. Quite often barking starts because the puppy has learnt that every time he goes in the car, there is a very pleasant exciting run at the end of it. So the first path to peace here is to ensure that some outings in the car do not result in a fun run. Drive to the shops and back home, drive round the streets for a quarter of an hour or so, and then home. Boring? Yes, but it works.

Try to avoid shouting "be quiet" as you are driving. Often this will serve the excite the puppy more, and encourage renewed barking. If the barking is caused because the puppy is excited by the traffic rushing by, or because he sees other dogs on the pavement, then here's where his crate comes in useful again. Cover it with a light cotton sheet so that he cannot see through the side windows.

DON'T SNATCH!

Because food is such a valuable resource, you may find that your puppy becomes over-anxious about getting his reward. When you are offering food from your fingers, he may well try to snatch it. This may seem quite harmless at first, but if he catches a child's fingers it may hurt. So it's a good ploy to teach him from very early on that he does not need to snatch.

Hold a piece of food in your fingers and close your fingers around it so that the puppy will be able to smell it, but not be able to take it. Allow him to sniff your fingers but keep them firmly closed over the food. Here you can give a cue of "off" if you want to, or say nothing at all. The instant he takes his nose away from your fingers, open them allowing him to take the food, and give the cue "take it". Praise him as he does so. If you have already taught him to wait a few seconds for his food when you put the bowl down, this cue will already be a familiar one. If you are clicker training, click as he takes his nose away, and let him take his reward.

STEALING FOOD

Many dogs are dustbins on legs, and given the opportunity will steal food. Remember the dog is an opportunist - he will eat whatever is available on the basis that tomorrow there may be none. Despite the fact that we feed our puppies and our dogs regularly, they are still programmed to react to some situations much as their wild ancestors did. Food is an extremely valuable resource, and the better it smells the more desirable it is. So leave a sandwich on the coffee table, and you can expect it to disappear. Put the chicken to cool on the work top, and it may not be there when you get back.

Puppies may not be able to reach the work tops initially, but they grow very quickly, and you might be surprised to see just how far up a puppy can reach if he stands on his back legs and leans the front ones on the coffee table or work top!

If you have one that discovers the delights of thieving, or who raids the kitchen bin on every possible occasion, then this is one of the few times when you go out of your way to give him a fright. But....and here's the important but, the fright has to be seen to result from his behaviour, and have nothing to do with you.

So set up the scenario. Leave some food temptingly available, but pile up some empty cans and boxes in such a way that as he grabs the food, the cans and boxes will clatter down round about him. One such fright may not be enough, but two or three most certainly will deter the would-be thief. This is far more effective than trying to catch him in the act and reprimand him.

STEALING SOCKS..AND OTHER THINGS!

Puppies quickly learn that picking something up and rushing down the garden provokes great interest and attention from owners. This may be no problem if it is his toy he has in his mouth, but if it is one of your best shoes, or some pretty underwear, it is less amusing.

So ignore him if he steals something, even if your every instinct is to rush after him shouting "Stop". If you attempt to retrieve it it becomes even more fun, and you may even find the puppy begins to growl and shake the item. Go to the fridge, cut some small pieces of cheese, or get some other strong smelling food which is not everyday fare, and call him in a pleasant, excited tone.

Show the treat plainly. As soon as he approaches, either with the trophy in his mouth or having dropped it to come running, give him the reward saying the cue "take it". If he still has the item in his mouth, take it saying "give" in a pleasant tone. Or if he has dropped it, walk quietly to it, pick it up and put it out of sight. Teaching the puppy to give items on cue is also good groundwork for teaching a retrieve later on.

If your puppy is one that responds strongly to toys, then have a very desirable toy for this express purpose. Let him play with it until he is bored, then put it quietly away for use on another occasion.

Be aware here that children find it a great game to chase the puppy when he runs off with something of theirs - and of course it's hugely exciting for the puppy to have the children in full cry behind him, all trying to retrieve the stolen items. Don't be surprised to find this happens while you are temporarily out of ear shot. Good fun for all, but not good training!

GROOMING

All dogs need regular grooming, just how frequently depends on the length of coat. Most puppies enjoy being groomed, especially if you throw in some gentle massage as well. It may seem unnecessary to groom a puppy coat, but if he learns young that it is pleasant to be brushed and combed you will obviate possible problems when he is larger and the coat longer and thicker.

Some dogs really dislike being groomed, and it can become a real battleground, but teaching the puppy to accept grooming early on brings benefits as do many other things taught early.

Every day pick up each foot gently, and give it a very gentle squeeze. Open his mouth gently and look at his teeth. Lift each ear flap. Check under his tail to ensure the anal area is clean. Then take a soft brush and brush his coat gently. If the puppy is restless hold a treat in one hand, or a favourite toy, and give just two or three strokes of the brush. Then a reward. Two or three more, and another reward. Ignore any attempts to chew the brush, but be sure not to reward if he does so.

Once he is comfortable with being brushed then start to give some gentle grabs and gentle tail pulls. Children are often unintentionally heavy handed, and the puppy that is accustomed to your gentle grabs will be less likely to react if a child grabs him or pulls his tail.

Cleaning the puppy's teeth is also a good habit to get him into. This too can be a battleground initially, so get a really soft brush (a toothbrush designed for very small children is good), and some special dog toothpaste. Lift his lip gently, give one or two strokes of the brush, and praise him. He will almost certainly chew at the brush at first, but be patient. Teaching him to accept his teeth being brushed will ensure you can keep his mouth and teeth in good order throughout his life.

FEAR OF OTHER DOGS

Strange as it may seem, some puppies and some older dogs are fearful of other dogs. After all, they are dogs - they should get on together. Puppies that have the opportunity to meet other puppies and dogs in those first vital eighteen weeks of life are much less likely to have problems. Sometimes we inadvertently cause the problem by protecting our puppy, picking him up if another dog appears, pulling the lead tight, or even shouting at the other dog. All of these actions serve to tell the puppy there is something to worry about, and the fear grows. It helps sometimes to keep in mind that puppies under six months give out scent signals (pheromones). All dogs recognise these scent signals, and very few will harm a puppy. But...there is always the exception, and it is wise to ensure as far as possible that initially at least, the puppy meets only dogs you know to be calm, friendly, and of course healthy.

If the worst happens, and your puppy does become very fearful, how best to cope? Sometimes puppies and dogs interact more easily if they are off lead, but with a young puppy there is a risk of him running off in fright, and even a reliable recall may fail to keep him out of possible dangers. So in the early stages of modification, use a lead for safety. Arrange to meet your friends on a side road where there will be less distraction. Initially pass on opposite sides of the road. Ignore any lunging or barking. Praise immediately it stops. Here you will find the use of a head collar (Gentle Leader, Kumfi Dog Alter, Halti) worth its weight in gold. This allows you to turn your puppy's head gently towards you, breaking eye contact with the oncoming dog. Often this will switch off any fearful response. Keep the lead loose, and try to be as relaxed as possible. Talk to him and praise him quietly while he is calm. Avoid speaking to him or touching him if he barks, pulls forward or tries to run away, as your actions will reward the unwanted response.

Build on this until you are able to pass each other with the dog and the puppy adjacent to each other. Praise quietly when he passes the other dog without any fuss. You can also give small food rewards, or employ a toy to distract him and to reward calm behaviour. Eventually you should aim to stop and talk to your friend with both dogs in a "sit" close together. If they attempt to sniff and greet each other, and it is a calm meeting, then allow this to happen.

Once you decide he is more able to cope then organise a meeting with other dogs in a safe area - a well fenced park or even a tennis court - just to ensure the safety of the puppy should he initially still show some fear.

FEAR OF VISITORS

Here again socialisation plays its part. A puppy that meets a wide variety of people - all ages, shapes, and sizes - in those first important weeks of life is unlikely to show fear of visitors. But even with good socialisation, a bad experience can mean the puppy becomes wary of them. So here we work to teach him that visitors are a good thing for a puppy. And, as discussed many times, food is very often the way to the puppy's heart.

Keep a pot of treats near the front door, and ask visitors to drop two or three as they arrive. Once they are seated, ask them to ignore the puppy and avoid looking at him. Give them some treats which they can toss gently towards the puppy still without looking at him. Allow the puppy to approach in his own good time, and then they can offer a few small treats on the flat of their hand, still not looking at him - eye contact can be scary. Once the puppy is approaching more readily then they can stroke him gently, talk to him quietly, and the large majority of puppies will soon recognise that visitors are to be welcomed.

In the event that the puppy continues to be fearful, then allow him to retreat to his crate when they arrive, leave the door open, and let him come out in his own time. He is free to come and go as he will, treats can be gently tossed near the crate, and once he feels more confident he is likely to come out of the crate and approach of his own accord. Softly softly is the key note here.

SAFETY WITH CHILDREN

Children and puppies usually have a natural affinity, but sometimes puppies are worried by their quick movements. Equally, some children are frightened of dogs, so some thoughtful introductions can bring about the situation of the children and the puppy happy in each other's company. Here you often have the start of a life-long love of dogs and other animals.

If there are no children in the household, then beg and borrow those of the neighbours. As outlined earlier under Socialisation, your puppy needs to meet children of all ages, from babies through to teenagers. The movements and voices are different at different ages, so the more experience of children the puppy has, the more confident he will be in their presence.

Ask the children to sit down initially, arm them with some food rewards, and allow the puppy to approach in his own time. Some will rush to the children eagerly, others may hold back and take time to approach. When he does, then each child can hold out his hand, keeping it flat, with a small treat visible. Ask them to move slowly at first, and once the puppy approaches, allow him to take the treat, talk to him and stroke him gently.

It's important always to supervise young children and puppies. Both are capable of becoming over-excited. The puppy may then mouth the hands or clothing of the child, or the child may inadvertently handle the puppy too harshly.

There is no reason why the children should not help with preparing the puppy's food, with his training, and most will enjoy going to puppy socialisation classes with him. If the lure of a puppy at home is irresistible, just think how much the children will enjoy playing and interacting with the six or eight puppies in class. Wonderful socialisation for the puppies, and fun for the children.

INTRODUCING OTHER PETS

Just how you set about introducing other pets depends on what species is involved. If you already have a dog or dogs in the house, then the puppy can meet them straight away, providing of course the dogs are in good health and up to date with vaccinations.

The first meeting of new dog and older dog needs some organisation - and this applies whether the newcomer is a puppy or past puppyhood. We tend to expect that automatically all dogs will meet and greet each other pleasantly, but this is not always the case. It can come as a shock if resident dog curls his lip and says "Thanks, but no thanks" to the squirming enthusiastic bundle of puppy. Keep in mind that puppies have been used to playing with their litter mates, and may rush up to the older dog, jumping and licking at his face, in such a manner that the phrase "where angels fear to tread" comes into mind. Even the most even tempered dog may resent this youthful enthusiasm.

Remember that dogs are born with the built-in ability to communicate with their own species, but they do need to refine and hone those skills. The curled lip and the growl that the older dog may give is a valuable lesson for the puppy. He will thereafter be more circumspect in his greetings, and this may save him a nip from a dog that is less tolerant than his new house mate. It's important to allow the older dog to chastise the puppy unless he becomes very rough with him. Puppies can quickly become little bullies, making the older dog's life miserable if you never allow the older one to teach him some manners.

Introductions are best carried out in the garden where the resident dog may feel less territorial than in the house. First ensure that the puppy has had an opportunity to empty his bladder, or excitement may cause him to eliminate when he meets the older dog. Puppy and dog should both be on leads, and allowed to approach each other. If the puppy is very young, between 8-11 weeks, then it is important to avoid him being frightened by the older dog. This is termed the "fear period" and a scare in this time tends to remain in the memory for life. Allow them to sniff each other, and then take both into the house so that the puppy can explore.

There are two ways of allowing dog and newcomer to become used to each other's presence. The first is simply to allow the puppy access to the same areas as you already allow the existing dog. This does mean that you need to be aware of the communication passing between the two dogs. Initially the older dog may seem rather unhappy - this is the time when you ask yourself if you have done the right thing, but wait a few days! He may take himself off to a place out of reach of the puppy, or he may seem rather withdrawn or restless. Usually this settles down in a few days, as dog and puppy learn to get along together, and you may well have the pleasure of finding them curled up together contentedly, or even sharing the same food bowl.

The second choice is to use a crate and to introduce the puppy to this by putting in his bedding and some toys. Let him go in and out of his own accord at first, but you can encourage him to enter by tossing in a few small food treats. Then gently close the door. Both puppy and dog can observe one another and their scents will become familiar. The older dog will not be plagued by an enthusiastic puppy when you are not around to supervise those early days, and the puppy can rest when he needs to. This can be a very easy way to introduce the puppy, always keeping in mind that he should not be in the crate for hours at a time.

Cats are a different matter and perfectly able to make their feelings obvious with a smack from a paw and an outraged hiss. Here you may find it more beneficial to pop the cat into his travelling cage, and allow him to get used the presence of the puppy. If you choose to let them meet more naturally, then ensure that the cat has an escape route, or you may have the cat climbing rapidly up the curtains or jumping up on the mantlepiece amid all those precious ornaments and the clock!

Other small mammals such as rabbits, guinea pigs and so on are best introduced in their cages where they and the puppy can get used to the sight and smell of each other. Cage birds may flutter and become agitated; if so cover the cage while the puppy is about and they too will become used to each other. It's important right from day one to begin to teach the puppy that chasing any other animals is strictly out of bounds. If he does so or attempts to do so, slip fingers into his collar and give a quick "ah ah" warning quietly, but firmly.

DIGGING

The garden is a real puppy paradise - a playground just made for four busy paws and equally busy teeth! Plants to pull up, holes to dig, flower pots to demolish, the odd slug for company (my own young bitch used to bring me snails as presents), birds to watch, a spot of pruning to do, a whirly full of washing to grab and run round in circles with. Oh yes, all manner of possibilities for the agile puppy mind exist in the garden. Although most of these things will not harm the puppy - though some plants are poisonous - we may not always welcome this enthusiastic gardener's assistant.

Distraction is the key to preventing the garden turning rapidly into a demolition site. Digging is a natural dog behaviour, so if possible fence or rope off an area of the garden, provide a sand pit, let the puppy see you bury some interesting toys and let him satisfy his urge to dig. Praise and encourage him, and use a negative "ah-ah" if he strays beyond the confines of his patch. Toys and bones can be buried time and time again, giving the puppy the fun of digging and finding them. If space is really at a premium, then a child's plastic sand pit can be bought for a few pounds and put to his use. Remember to cover a sand pit at night or you may have unwelcome nocturnal visitors using it.

CAR SICKNESS

Car sickness is not uncommon in puppies. It may be due to the motion of the car, but it may also be due to the fact that the puppy's experience of the car has not been pleasant. First he has been taken from his mother and litter mates and transported in a swaying, strange smelling, noisy vehicle to an unfamiliar place. His next experience of the car may be to the veterinary surgery where he has an injection, which may momentarily hurt him. Car sickness often passes once the puppy learns that at the end of the car ride there is a lovely fun run in the park or fields, but that is several weeks away.

Try feeding him his meals in the car with it stationary to build up a happier association. If you are using a crate and intend to use this also in your car, then feed him in the crate inside the car. After a few meals have been given in this way, it is time to drive a very short distance, and on return take him out of the car and play a game with him. Each experience should be short and pleasant. If the sickness persists it is worth giving him a small drink of glucose and water before a journey, which often settles a queasy small stomach. An alternative is ginger capsules obtainable from the chemist which do seem to work miracles with some sufferers. (These work with people too.)

CHEWING

Again chewing is a natural behaviour. It relieves painful gums while the puppy is teething, it helps the second teeth to bed down in the jaw properly, it keeps teeth and gums clean, and many dogs - including adult dogs - enjoy chewing for the sheer sake of it.

So here it pays to teach the puppy what he can and cannot chew. Of course, it helps enormously if you can persuade the family to put things away that might more usually get deposited on the floor, but you need to provide plenty of chewing toys for the puppy and for the dog he will become. There are plenty to choose from and they come in all shapes, sizes and prices. Go for good quality that will not be chewed to pieces in ten minutes flat and renew them if you spot any signs of damage.

Encourage the puppy to play with these and chew them. If at any time he approaches forbidden items, then use your firm "ah ah", and immediately give him something he can chew to his heart's content. You may find that the puppy quickly learns when he has something forbidden - your facial expression and body language will tell him - and when this happens he may well run away in an attempt to keep possession of it. It can be tempting to chase after him, but of course this becomes a great game - and one he will win every time. A way of coping with this eventuality is outlined in "Stealing Socks...and other things!"

TAKING POSSESSION OF THE SOFA

If the puppy has been taught from early on what is and what is not allowed - remember setting those boundaries - then this kind of resource guarding should not occur. But at times this does happen and it is easy to fall into the trap of being confrontational in trying to remove him. Pulling and pushing him down quickly becomes a battle of wills. Next time he will resist more strongly.

There is an easier way! Go into the kitchen, cut a few slivers of cheese or something else strong smelling and tasty. Come back with them visible in your hand, call the puppy, and offer the reward. Immediately he gets down, ask him to sit or give a paw, and reward him with a piece of cheese or your chosen treat.

Occasionally the puppy may sit tight. If so, don't despair. Eat the cheese, or whatever food you have selected, with every sign of enjoyment. It is a foolish puppy who does not respond when you then call him off again!

Much the same tactics can be employed if the puppy is in the garden, and showing no signs of wanting to come in. Go out, get his attention, and toss either a food reward or a toy into the kitchen. He will run in and you have achieved what you wanted without any chasing, shouting, or getting impatient. Reward and praise him.

Use similar non-confrontational approaches if any small problems do develop. Giving the puppy the opportunity to respond as you want, rewarding and praising him wins the day.

RECALL PROBLEMS

Teaching your puppy to come to you in the house and garden, well before his vaccination programme is complete and he is able to go out into the world, gives you the best chance of avoiding recall problems. But it is not a cast iron guarantee, and once the puppy discovers all those wonderful smells, other dogs to play with, and people to go and have a chat to, you may well find that the willing puppy that came hot foot at home has suddenly become selectively deaf.

Maddening? Oh yes! But here is yet another occasion when patience wins the day. The cardinal rule is not to lose your temper even if you have stood in the rain for half an hour while the puppy cavorts around merrily. No matter how long it takes when he returns, praise, smile and reward him as you clip on his lead. After all, he has returned. Punish him and the next recall will be slower, and the one after that slower still. No puppy will want to return to his owner to be shouted at or smacked. This is a real test of your patience.

Try to get in the habit of calling him once and once only. If you call again and again he will very quickly learn that he does not have to return when you call, because you will call him again. Turn and walk away at which most puppies will follow you. You can then reward and praise him. If he does not follow, then you can try one of several things. Hide - no puppy wants to lose sight of his owner. Or sit down on the ground and pretend to be examining something really really interesting. Curiosity may well bring him running. Make squeaky crying noises. Again this is likely to bring him hot foot. If all of these fail, then go very quietly towards him, clip on the lead, and turn in the direction you want to go. No need for words, the action and your silence will tell him this is not wanted behaviour.

An excellent way of forming a very good association with your recall cue is to release the puppy - in a safe area of course - and call him frequently and very enthusiastically. Reward him every time with a small food reward, and release him to play again. Repeat this as often as possible while you are out walking, so that returning to you is always exciting and pleasant, especially in these important early weeks.

Sometimes it is necessary to use a long line attached to his collar to ensure you can guide him gently back to you if all other ploys fail. Remember always to give the cue pleasantly, guide him in, and reward him then release him to play again.

Here we come to the end of the list of possible puppy problems, and easy ways in which to overcome them. Don't despair if you are having problems. Advice is always available from your veterinary surgeon, from an experienced instructor, or from a behaviour counsellor with whom your vet can put you in touch.

Puppyhood is a fleeting period in which you and your puppy learn each other's ways and how to live together. Your puppy may spring a surprise or two, but kind, gentle training and handling overcomes most problems.

Enjoy your puppy!